All and Only
The First Word and...
The Last

Martha Kilpatrick

This is the author's Statement of Faith:

Jesus Christ, the only begotten Son of God,
came in the flesh, shed His Holy Blood on the
Cross at Calvary for the sins of the world.
He is Lord of the Universe, King of Kings.

...and I am His Shulamite.

Contents

Introduction

The enigma of suffering.
The perpetual question is a challenge
not only to the power of God but to His very nature:

how can a good God allow suffering?

One who has the power to do anything at anytime...
that One is sovereign.

Even if He doesn't use that power. To withhold power is
still to possess it.

There is an explanation and it lies with a

benevolent Creator

as His sensible secret...

That is enough.

The lusting mind gropes for explanations...
"I will trust if I can only understand."

By asking the question we are demanding that God win –
not only our approval – but our consent.
We must authorize His actions.

If I were God, I'd make it all so clear, explain myself so I'd
be loved...
But God is not a God who stoops

to get permission for His actions.

When the terrible-what-happens occurs,

our hold on His absolute dominion is attacked,
and our hope is enfeebled that
He is good, greatly good.

And what we really believe comes snarling out.

I asked a missionary candidate,
"Does your school teach that God is sovereign?"

"Oh, yes, God is all-powerful."

Powerful we all agree. But sovereign?

Sovereign is not the same as powerful.
          Powerful could… if it would.
          Sovereign IS.

Isn't it true that
          if He is so much as one event less than sovereign,

          He is then NOT sovereign?
             We would have to use another word.

By the dictionary sovereign means: paramount,
          supreme sovereign,
          complete independence and self government.

          Sovereign is a word of absolutes.

Though full explanation is beyond the comprehension of
          finite human minds
               there is an answer.

          Explanation   means I unveil my reasons.
          Answer   means only that I have a reason.

The answer is given
             not thought through
             not figured out
             not deduced… by the minds of men.

The answer is simply given in His Word.

I AM

God identified Himself to Moses as… I AM.

What a strange way to say it.

Nothing unsaid … in the most amazing self disclosure
God had said it all.

I AM   All

All there is

All you need

Anything, everything

Only

The Trees

The Tree of Knowledge was
      the Tree of Ignorance.
There is Only One who knows.

Scripture is clear. From beginning to end.

God is. And He is God. There is no other.

It is we who put events into categories with labels.
Thus we live by the Tree of Death:
man's pompous belief that
he can tell the difference between
good and evil...

Sometimes

the kiss of a friend is betrayal,

an untimely death is on time,

a gentle sheep hides a vicious fang.

When will we see how small is our seeing?

And trust...

Looking out into the world
(my little one and that vast one) I see

immense forces at work... powers in combat.
Men kill men. Nations now can kill ALL men...

Despots imprison and dominate.

Satan is there. His powers
　　　　swirling, … seeming to win.

Then there's me. I can destroy. I can hurt.

Finally, God. Is there any power left to His disposal?

Yes, there are vying powers. Huge and fearsome powers.
Bigger than me, bigger than the earth! And as I look at what
　　can be seen…
　　　　　　　　I see them.

But when I look long in God's Word,
　　　there is nothing more plain,

　　nothing more repetitive than this:

　　　God is in final charge of all things.

　　　He has the Last Word and the one who has

　　　the Last Word has *all* the power.

Abraham

God will Sovereignly Accomplish
what He asks of you.
All by Himself.

A man must be called.
He doesn't choose his place in God's chronicles
                    nor the timing of it.

The pathways of his story also are mapped out,
                    by God, not himself.

Abraham, singled out by God, chosen
          among heathen idolaters
                    to know and follow I AM.
                    To know by following...

He was elected to a place, a time and
                    a particular demonstration of God.
                    And so are you.

He was selected to father nations
          but God made sure that it was

                    humanly impossible, divinely improbable.

Long before God performed this, He spoke it.

He is God over All, Only Ruler and Controller.
          When He speaks the very universe
                    heaves to accomplish it.

Natural laws collapse before the sound of
His Transcendent Voice.
Human wills spend their fight, then bow.

His resounding Word breaks and creates,
makes and separates.

And nothing holds it back,
not even humanity's bungling stupidity.

By the bitter education of error, Abraham learned that when
God spoke it was sovereignly accomplished.

How could Sovereignty speak and it NOT come to pass?

But it takes a while to see... God as God.
To discover that what He promises
only He can deliver.
God never asked for Abraham's help,
only his surrender...

But because he thought God needed assistance,
Abraham had long years to eat the acrid fruit
of forcing God's promise into existence
before it was ripe.

His putrid creation of God's Idea
sapped him to the last ounce of hope.
Drained his marriage, too.

Abraham eventually learned to pray instead of perform.
To wait rather than run,
see God and not himself.

And most of all, he discovered *how to receive:*

To receive the all encompassing
blessing of God... without deserving it.

To relinquish what he loved most, to receive
it back alive from divinely-ordered death.

To accept without protest his frightening inadequacy
either to effect God's will or
even to keep from trying to do so!

Isaac was conceived when the man was
destitute of trying to support God's plan,
by the collapse of his own prowess
and was left with nothing but... stark faith
in the Only One Who has power.

When a man is reduced to the
embarrassing level of simple receiving
then God's promise has no obstacle of fulfillment...

no strutting man to take credit for
what God did all by Himself.

But no one will ever volunteer to live by
   the dire vulnerability of receiving.

  It's too, too naked.

  He must be shamed into it by the
   hopelessness of every other possibility.

He must be disabled out of his determination to fulfill
  a vision he did not originate.

   Weakness is man's final invitation

    for which God unendingly waits.

Jacob

If a man embraces Sovereignty it will
mean that someone other than
he is God.

Jacob, man of action. He would wrest his destiny out on his
own, thank you. He needed no help from God to effect
God's plan.

Human dynamo — making it happen.

Any means justified the end and he used any means to
gain the blessing promised to him in the womb.
God had promised it so stealing it was not immoral.

The human sliding scale of integrity.

But Jacob was sovereignly chosen so

no matter what wreck he made, God fixed it.
No matter where he ran, God ran with him.
However low he sank, God went there also.
Whatever problem he had was the affair of God.

There was no Divine Rebuke and no rejection. Oh yes, there
was chastening. There were consequences.

But present more were
Absolute Commitment and Unequivocal Presence...
to the consummate end.

Sovereignty is a true friend.

Jacob was finally tired of his pitiful management

and ready to face the brother he cheated.

He was a man broken on the
beam of his own striving

but in such desperation, such frantic need
of God that his grip was iron and his
final strength no longer
human achievement
of Divine Ends

but only

the power of critical necessity:
an urgent hold on God that would
not let Him go...

All other powers were gone:
scheming, working, conquering.
These powers had wearied him
and ultimately failed to bring him to the
destiny for which he had sold
his soul's honor.

But by that final power of brutal desperation
at last he touched
the only human strength that
moves God to take over....
raw need.

God had been *with him* watching,
    waiting through every shortcut,

        committed to the man even in
        his rank independence

        but now Jacob vacated the Chair and

        let God have His Rightful Throne.

So Jacob, by unending crisis, was transformed into Israel.
    The man *of* God became the man *IN* God.

        And that is two entirely different men.

        The very core essence of the man had been

        transformed by

        the final comprehension of…

        his dismal failure at being God.

        I AM.

Joseph

There aren't many Josephs.
We would rather pet our
bitterness than wear a crown.

And that is precisely our choice...

It's funny: the one who seeks no "whys"

> knows... eventually... the answer to the
> questions he needed not to ask.

And only that kind of person ever finds out.

Joseph, that magnificent hero, became such
> because he pushed past

the obsession with "why" and dealt instead with "how."

> How can I please God?
> How can I serve God?

If ever a man had the hostile right to ask "why"

> wouldn't it have been Joseph?

> A favored son.

> A faithful son.

Clean...
> malleable yet strong
> enough to report the wrongs
> of his brothers... when asked to.

Cruelly rejected

for his God-originated dream

and for his sterling character.

We hear no railing screech of "Why, God?"
A simple setting to the task at hand.

The question of Joseph: "What is your will here?"

The human question is "why?"
"Give me all Your reasons and then, maybe then I will
follow You."
The legitimate question,
the one that can be known is "what?"

God's "what" is "Do the task at hand. Live the life you find."
And Joseph did it.

Only to suffer again, not from sin but
because he wouldn't sin!

We would have screeched, "What good is it?
God is not fair and there is no justice!"

Oh, but I AM.

In the hell-hole where any reasonable person gives up because

> his "why," saps all his innards,

> the caged Joseph asked again… "what?"

>> "What is Your will?
>> What is my task?"

"Do the task at hand. Live the life in which you are trapped.
> Do it well in the faith that I have a Divine Aim."

> And Jospeh did.
> Even there.

The question is not "why" but "what" and
> through the devoted acceptance of what God wants,
> the "why" of His purpose emerges.

In some off-the-record unveiling to his heart, Joseph came to see

> God's unimaginable but brilliant purpose.
> We know the end of the story. Joseph didn't.
> For him it had been a blank mystery,
> a puzzle he couldn't have solved.
>> It was God's secret. Only He could reveal it.
>> And He did.

"God sent me ahead of you to preserve for you a remnant
on earth and to save your lives by a great deliverance."
> Genesis 45:7

He knew. Joseph knew why.
It was a purpose so great, so heroic,
he was willing to have suffered for its fulfillment.

Trauma creates a dilemma with God, not only with life.
It throws His character into dispute,
    His power into doubt, His love into question.
    Suffering twists our view of God so He seems
        both small and inept.

Suffering doesn't need explanation.
The experience of it calls for healing not reason because
    suffering splits you in two,
    creates a breach between you and
        your own existence.
The rigid stance you take against your personal pain
        straining to erase your event,
        and not to include it in your present,
        makes you your own murderer.

For your suffering has a life of its own, full of unborn ideas,
        pulsing with mystery,
        rich with potential to solve your future suffering,
        and – most amazing – your past as well.

Your suffering holds the secrets to your appointed lot and is
therefore the hiding place of your power.

You must value your suffering enough to
coax its treasure into your using.

In the end

Joseph found out why.

He'd been in school, the making of a ruler, whose
power saved many lives.

The "why" unmasks itself only to the faithful.

For Joseph, I AM had been enough.
God could have. God didn't.

So God had good reason.

Most men never make it to the end… to see.

Their furious "whys" have gnawed their mammoth potential

down to a tiny bitter nub of ineffectiveness…

long before the end.

Balaam

The man who doesn't let God rule him
is lowered beneath the donkey who does…

God is so much God that no person can thwart Him,
> no person can fool Him and
> no one can use Him.

Balaam is a name that stands for greed – through the ages
of eternity it will so stand.
> Shameful corruption of a pure calling.

The king of the Moabites wanted to pay Balaam to curse a
protected Israel. And he would pay well to secure that
curse. Being a valid prophet, Balaam asked God.
> The answer was "no," clear and unequivocal.

So the king upped the price. Balaam asked again and the
answer seemed to have changed to "yes." When you ask
God a second time, it exposes that you want something
more than you want His will.

And Sovereign Lord will often release you to the thing.

> You now have to walk it out.
> It nests in your heart so you must see its
> > sorry conclusion.

It's not His will but it is His permission. However,
> make no mistake:

> His will will prevail... with you or without you.

So Balaam's donkey corrected him.
>
> Balaam's lust to go was such that he didn't realize
> his pride had just been insulted
> by God's use of
> > the dumbest and basest of animals.

Balaam drew a sword to kill the animal
> that would dare to stop his prosperous adventure.

Donkeys and angels belong to God.
> They serve Him… faithfully.
> It is only humanity that is so foolish
> as to know better than God.

Still God let him go, even sent him. See?
> Sovereignty does not mean unmitigated control.

> God's purpose is not the slightest threatened by
> > our failure to get in it.
> Nor do lawless actions limit in any way
> > His ultimate end.

He had pronounced Israel blessed.
> No man could out-pay or out-pray that blessing.
> A man's curse over what God blesses only
> returns back to him,
> > in dreadful fullness.

Balaam, man of money, tried but couldn't curse. When he
opened his prophet's mouth he could only pronounce
a victorious benediction to Israel
and a clear prophecy about the Christ.

The man who can be bought may be anointed but he is not
absolute. Payment for God's Word can be a terrible
corruption of the man of God... Be careful. Be careful.

You can't use God's enemy for your
own aggrandizement nor
evil for your good.
Such pay is vile.
God Himself pays his own servants.
No need to compromise.

Wait for the miracle of the raven and the widow's cruse.

God will use men. He has that right.
He may spend, wreck, and send a man.

But He is honorable and that one will be
rewarded entirely and
sustained absolutely.
The Only God will not tolerate being exploited to
increase a man's stature or his purse

Public exposure will come upon that man's motive and
condemnation not only from God but men as well.

As are prophets and donkeys, the power of a curse is
        entirely subject
                        to the wishes of the

                Great I AM.

Saul

Haughty little kings may strut, prance,
and run amok,
but the Eternal still rides their backs and
holds the reins.

God crowns kings. They reign for Him.

> Should they cease to reign for Him, they are then
> dethroned.

Saul was a grand specimen of a man but of
> sorry mettle as a king.
>> He began well, but lasted
>> only briefly as Sovereign Choice.

King was not enough for him. He would be priest as well.
Victor was not sufficient. He would be God as well:
> decreeing who would live and who would die,
>> by the deliberate ignoring of God's ruling.

> Giving witless mercy where The Father did not,

> to the sworn enemy of His purpose.

Though he kept the power and the position,
> he'd lost the Favor of the One who enthrones man.

> So his crown was hollow and jewelless.

Enough, God said. But kings are God's.
> He *will* use them for His own ends. He will.

So Saul became the instrument of Divine Supremacy
        to train the successor he hated.
        This was God's original intent and Saul
        would fulfill it positively or negatively...
        but discharge it to the ultimate, he would!
So David learned from Saul *how not* to rule as king

        by the instruction of...
        his suffering.

This is just as valuable and fundamental
        as when the role model
        is ideal.

        God prevails.

        His Brilliant Design is fulfilled either way.

        <u>This</u> is Sovereignty!

David

One only praises
whose God is God.

David praised.

Never before had a man worshipped like David.
Maybe never since.

He praised

seven times a day,
continually.
In the midst of trouble.
In and after tragedy.
After guilt and its punishment,
after blessing.

Emotionally, creatively, poetically… physically!

Oh, yes, we are commanded to praise. We are called to and
created for that activity.

Yet do we praise as an instant rule of response?

For a burned treasure?
A stolen reputation?
An untimely death?
The unfair, the unkind,
the ridiculous, the excruciating?

Oh, yes, Satan is there and he must be resisted,
even silenced.

Yet is that not a secondary rather than a
    primary concern?
Is not his activity limited to the boundaries God sets?
Does not Job's story prove this forever?

Oh, yes, there are consequences to my sin.
    I reap the evil I sow.
But doesn't God alone determine the extent, the scope of
that reaping? Didn't he do so with David? And David
worshipped in acceptance of that cost.

I can only worship and
I will only praise
        to the exact proportionate degree of my belief that
            God is the Final Determiner of all.
            To that degree I will worship... the real God.

Man worships. The question is not whether he worships for
that is his unconscious purpose.
        The question is *what* does he worship?

Worship is the centrality of every life.
        You worship what owns you and you choose —
            quite deliberately — what does own you.

We are all orphans seeking a Father... to meet our need.
And what we perceive holds the means of sustenance, that
source is where we begin to build our sacred altar and call
it "father".

We build an altar at the foot of the fountain of supply,
      whatever we perceive that is…
            be it man, job, idea, object.

But what we need has power over us and
      that power is frightening and unsettling
      for the vulnerability it exposes.

So this is the basis for every person's choice of god:
      Something in life, you believe is essential.
      And that essential-need has power over you.
      And what has power over you, you fear,
            deeply do you fear.

A man reserves his worship for what possesses
      highest supremacy.
            Nobility doesn't enter into it.
            It's raw power that captures us and
                makes us subjects.

And what you fear you worship.
      You may hate the object you worship.
      You may chafe under it, but it is still worship.

We are mistaken to believe that what we love is what we
worship. Not so. It is possible to hate with grim force the
thing that towers over us, but still be caught in the
veneration of it.
What you need is what has power over you.
      What has power is what you fear.
      And what you fear, you deify.

You are owned by whatever you need and by that which you fear. And what owns you becomes your god.

No matter your testimony. No matter your words.
No matter your opinion of that to which you give
obeisance.

You give your life to the object of your worship.
And you will die for your object as well.
You live and die for that which you believe
holds your life in the balance.

What you need, you fear.
What you fear, you worship.
What you worship, you serve… and die for.

The same holds for man. If you suffer constant fear of man, then man is your god. If your terror is of poverty then poverty you will serve. And so on and on.

David learned Who was sovereign in the treacherous hills of Israel. He discovered the God who had more power than the bear and the lion. So when Goliath threatened, David was not afraid! The God who empowered him to meet the beasts, would rule the giant.

And it was so!

David's courage could be attributed to the size of his concept of God's power to rule.

Courage isn't a character quality.
It is the result of what you believe has power.

David's faith in a Sovereign Lord took him into battle
and brought him victory.
But the mad tyrant, Saul, came close to killing him and with
his monarch's powerful throne intimidated David.
And his sovereignty foundation was shattered by
the fear of death that took him.

His courage left him and he ran to hide.
His honesty left him and his lie brought the death
of 85 men! "Men who wore the linen ephod."
His dignity went down with it until he
took to saving himself by slobbering in his beard.

You will grovel for your idol, your fear-object.
You will... and you will become just like it, too.

But somewhere in those barren hills,
the hounded fugitive settled it.

No change in Saul to prove God big. No vindication of
David's innocence. Somehow though, he found his
Sovereign Lord again and the peace from accepting His
strange ways of control.
He recovered his worship, and with it his heroism to
once again battle great powers... and win.

He never lifted his hand again to protect himself, to
straighten out the mess, nor even to kill the king when he
could easily (and perhaps justifiably) have done so. His
Great Master was Lord of all. He could and would oversee
his release.

Who can imagine the throes of David's thrashing it out?
>   Who could fathom his dealings and communion
>   with God in the wastelands to lay hold again of
>   his faith?

In later years, as King with power to kill, he knew that a foul
mouth that cursed him wrongly... was sent from God. And
God was able to bless David through evil as surely as
through good because
>   He was thwarted by nothing, stopped by no one.

Again, when his own son laid siege to David's throne, he left
it all to God, left the City – not to fight – but to leave the fray
to God's determining,

>   yielding his crown to God's protection alone.

One level of faith lays hold, grabs and grips. And that is
good faith. But another level of faith relinquishes entirely to
Almighty God and that is higher faith. Higher faith in a
Bigger God.

David was a praiser because His God was God,
big enough to rule and good enough to be
right in His ruling.

>   His God was sovereign.
>   But He was also good.

Esther

GOD prepares His Sovereign Solution
and hides it
in the very middle of the crisis,
long before it rises.

History lies not in fists of forceful kings but in
      the imploring hands of one who prays.

History belongs to God and He can change its entire course
      on the effect of one small life.

Esther was such a one, an obscure maiden
      imprisoned under a barbarous king.
      By her beauty cursed to slavery in his harem.

But a Sovereign God is not limited by what limits us.
      The imperfect situation is merely
          His stage of Triumph,
      the test of His Ascendancy.

God's favor can make you invisible or
      mark you as a beacon.
      That Divine preference of one person over another
      is based solely on His predestined choice.
      Not on worth or merit... or preferential love.

Esther walked out her little life with excellence and
simplicity, deferring always to those who ruled her and
      never dreaming the import of every move she made.
      Shy and always unassuming,
      she was forced to let herself be placed in
      the middle of a dangerous kingdom.
      In such a place she became a woman
          careful with her steps.

Esther let herself be parented by the uncle of adoption.
Allowed another's older wisdom to guide her.

Esther let herself be helped... taught, and as such she was
given the eunuch's secrets that earned her favor.

And time... time is the worthy price for developing
the spirit of a woman.

Six months with oil of myrrh,
the bitter substance of suffering.
Taking time to accept the suffering of her life –
what appeared to be its complete loss into a
hopeless nothingness. No way out!
Without her people and without a life of
any free choices.

What suffering she swallowed and
how she allowed it to gentle her!
When she finished her work of grieving
and let God choose her place... then

she spent six months with
"sweet spices and perfumes
for the purifying of the women – "

Fragrance doesn't rise from suffering.
A perfumed life exudes from surrender to God's
hand of limitation and only this is
a waft of sweetness,
intriguing by being rare.

Her adorning was not in flashy devices.

True beauty lies in simplicity...
     from divesting not acquiring.
Real elegance comes from a private heart of quiet mystery.
     Withholding more than giving.

She wore the dignity and grace of a queen, made so
     by God in some lovely crucible, veiled and terrible.

The king did not choose her, he merely recognized her.
     Who had been just one of many, became *the one*.
So Esther took her place in God's order...
     exalted through surrender.

She learned to be apart from her people and alone with her
secret of Jewish identity. A woman surrounded by numbers
and numbers of women
          yet who was incredibly alone.
          And she entered that solitude, that
          terrible isolation,
          with the internal submission – to God –
          that makes for nobility.

Her particular brilliance, that she always
     stayed in her place.
          By intense acceptance she had
          the power to see her boundaries and
          tolerate their limitations with quietness.
          Never overstepping or underplaying.

Truly, she died to her own destiny, never dreaming that by
that very perishing she was at its threshold.

Because she gave up power over her own life,
      she was entrusted with the Power
      to save the nation which was to
            mother the Christ child.

The power she possessed was not only the power of her
position, (that power is obvious).

      Her hidden power was inherent, the inner strength
of abdication… the great power of surrender to
            the gusts of God's changing winds.

Any and all have natural strength to seize.
      Few have wrung out the capacity to abdicate.

And even fewer understand that in that relinquishment
God's Sovereignty has no limitation, by having no rival.

He can expose a murder plot to just the right person.
He can give a king insomnia and guide his hand to a book
of records. And He can give an insignificant maiden a
crucial and pivotal role in the move of history:

        prepare her for – "such a time as this."

The crisis came. With her people threatened with extinction,
the sole power of their salvation lay with Esther.

Her natural reticence made her shrink but her
      acquired valor made her bow once again.
Bow to the most awful danger she had yet faced:
      to reveal her secret and have to share the
           fate of her people's annihilation.

Her position alone did not secure the
      king's automatic favor.

He was a monarch burned by a public shame
      at the hands of the insurgent Vashti.

           He was not approachable.

So she and her maids fasted in silent despearation.
And Wisdom came, advising her to give
      before she asked.

      To exalt the man who had imprisoned her.
      To acknowledge his God-given power with
           reverence.
      To "feed" his secret hunger.

To display her own splendor for the sake of
      his legitimate pride. She gave her best
     glory of womanhood
          to him, for him.
           The thing Vashti had refused to do.

She took her distilled life, gathered its hidden riches,
      and revealed herself fully, without reserve,
         to him in the presence of his
            watching world.

       Esther understood his need from her before she
          required her own to be met.

She acknowledged his crown and
      honored his throne
         before he crowned her with the scepter
          of half the kingdom.

She earned, I say EARNED, his favor before she asked for
her own.

Bowing in humble surrender,
      she gave him his due of perfect freedom,
         not dictating or forcing his decision.

      She knew he was... King!
      And she let him be so,
      conceding to his vast power over her –
      placing her literal life in his reigning hand.

And he gave her all she asked and more. Killed her enemy
instead of her people and gave her uncle-father, the
position closest to the throne.

Such is the power of a woman
who abandons herself to God and
the life He chooses for her:

Power of influence to change the flow of history
in God's direction.

For to give up power is be visited by the
Intervening Presence

of the One who has All Power...

and who rules rulers.

Job

A man can face suffering only
if he wrings it out in naked honesty with God…
not man,
not Satan.

Satan asked for Job.
I AM, the Protecting Force agreed.
Why would I AM do such a thing?
Job's friends knew why. Some dark and secret crime was
surely in Job, who deserved his suffering
or he wouldn't be suffering.

God, displeased with friends who dealt in proud whys,
in human explanations of divine inexplicables...
never justified Himself.

It was not an issue of sowing-and-reaping,
of justice, of cause-and-effect.

It was simply God's choice for Job.

When you are God, you don't owe anyone an
explanation of Yourself. Not anyone.

God simply chose Job's experiences.

Instead of answering questions of a striving man,
God asked a few questions of His own.

"Job, where were you when I WAS?"

"Job, who are you to ask why of the One who
made all?"

"Job, do you think you can tell me anything
I don't know?"

Those questions, those terrible questions showed Job the
gap between his intellect and God's. He shriveled from this
recognition and... saw God, really saw WHO HE IS for the
first time.

Job's friends live on... forever finding imagined whys in the
story. "It was Job's pride," but God Himself had said there
was no flaw in the man.

We will have our answers
even if we have to make them up.

Job's friends are ever lustfully unsatisfied with mysteries.
God's final answer to the matter was, "I AM (and that means
sovereign).
That's all I have to say."

Read the book backward. Read it forward, it still comes out
that God simply said I AM WHO I AM.

Job's was introduced to a Tremendous God.
His God was so little that He could only bless Job out
of blessing. Job didn't know he needed a God who was big
enough to bless him out of great catastrophe.

Job's fear was that I AM was not able to protect him,
and his world.
Job's God wasn't absolute.

And God loved Job enough to magnify Himself
before the man.

When he suffered and blessings went, God's character came
into question. So it is with us.

In talking about the most frightening creature on earth, God
argued for His supremacy, having made that creature. Job's
fear in life, of life, was keeping him from a higher worship.
God didn't consider his fear a condemnable wrong, merely
human ignorance and so

God resolved his fear, called him to fear only...
the Sovereign One.

I AM. No other is.

Not the crocodile.
Not man.
Not Satan.
Not Job.

Habakkuk

In the living experience of I AM,
"whys" shrivel into
boring irrelevance.

Habakkuk sat in a powerless heap,
>	a witness to the bloodshed, injustice, idolatry,
>	and wanton destruction of Judah at the hands
>		of godless Chaldeans.

When he got sick of it he did what any honest man does. He questioned the absence of God.
>	He asked Why, What and How long?

The difference between Habakkuk and others is this: he deliberately hurled the insults to God Himself. We usually complain about an impotent God to each other and rumble about His failures in secret to our own counsel. The everyday type of person is without
>	the integrity to face Him and
>	the courage to hear Him out.

But Habakkuk roared his moral outrage. "Justice never prevails," he said. "Destruction and violence are before me."

I AM answered quickly. But instead of pacifying the indignant man He loved, God proceeded to incite him further. He shocked Habakkuk by telling him a thing "never heard of before."

>	The savage nation out to destroy Judah had been sent deliberately by the Controlling Hand of God.

The wicked sent against the righteous to make them more righteous? The evil given predetermined power over God's people, a cruelty sent for the express purpose...
of suffering?
Habakkuk's idea of justice was shaken.
"How could You, who are innocent of wrong
use that same wrong for Your purposes?"

So the man interrogated His Feeble God for His inaction and began to accuse Him of being untrue to His own character. And God loved the fight.

Some will never say to God's face
what they imagine He doesn't hear in their hearts.

Now Habakkuk climbed upon the ramparts to watch and listen. He gave God opportunity to answer. Few will do that. "I will look to see what he will say to me."
And he set himself to wait.

What came was the certain promise of Divine Justice from the very mouth of Justice Himself:
The question was not "whether," only "when."
"Though the vision (of justice) tarry, wait for it
for it will surely come and will not tarry."

Justice is not made up of what "I" deem fair. Rectitude is what God ordains.
I AM... justice.
And justice delayed is not justice denied.

"The Lord is in His Holy temple." God is on the throne.
>   No one has ever usurped that throne. No one ever
>   will. Or ever could. No one thwarts Him, stops Him
>   or stumps Him.

"Let all the earth be silent before Him."
>   Man has nothing true to say against God and no
>   advice for Him. Because He is I AM, shut up.

God is God... ruling and omnipotent.
>   He can do whatever, whenever and for
>   whatever unstated purpose He deems right.

The man who wrestles with God always comes out with a
drastic life change. But the man who rails about Him
becomes cemented
>   in his doubting opposition.
>   He is left... alone... to think he's right.

God loves an honest battle.
>   He has no amenity for cowards.
>   He wins. He always wins.
>   This also Habakkuk knew beforehand.
>   He set himself on the rampart to be corrected
>   and wanted to be so.

God Almighty is never wrong. He bests you always.
>   Expect it, but in wonderful defeat you touch
>   His burning glory and bitter suspicions
>   about Him are purged.

God comes to the man who seeks His counsel and in that,
the answer
>is ever and only... Himself. This is who I AM.
>>Sovereign.
His Towering Presence shook this man and put him in his
smallness. To study God is to think you have mastered Him.
>But to meet Him is to be decimated.
>Habakkuk was faint in body,
>>his obdurate flesh stricken.

Shattered by His Words and Presence, Habakkuk was
reduced to naked faith in a Breathtaking God.

A man doesn't acquire faith. He is reduced to it...
>by humiliation.

>No longer would poverty divide him from His God.
>No more would trouble disturb his certainties.
>And no more would he mistrust the Throne.

The division between his emotions and his beliefs,
dissolved. The gap from the seen to the unseen, bridged.

Habakkuk burst forth in exuberant recognition.
>A Magnificent God, a Flaming Force,
>Utterly potent in the heavens:

"Sun and moon stood still in the heavens
at the glint of your flying arrows,
at the lightning of your flashing spear."

And upon the earth, no less a Fearsome God:

"He stood and shook the earth;
He looked, and made the nations tremble.
The ancient mountains crumbled
and the age old hills collapsed."

The man who has met "I AM" – face to face –
knows all he needs to know
and afterwards, can only joy his way through life.

Jonah

Every person is a living tale of God's sovereignty
but few – oh, very few –
are finished scripts of His vindication…

Free choice and sovereign rule.
It seems an insoluble contradiction…

We can't stomach both at the same time so we go
     back and forth.

Though God IS sovereign (through Christ's cross having
taken back His creation) He has limited Himself within His
own rights.
     He won't violate a man's priceless free will.

The great gift of the Cross (after forgiveness) is the
magnanimous gift of choice. It is true freedom under God,
real and actual.

Autonomy is fact.

However, every choice, *no matter how small,* is
     an issue of life and death.

We are blissfully blind as to that. We see "either, or."
If I don't take this road, why I can always take that one.

Not so with God. He has one Plan and no
     second arrangement.
A man who chooses an alternate road loses God. Utterly.

God's will admits no substitute no matter how good its fruit.
He is *not* flexible.

The choice is there. It's real, but it is only dual, not multiple.
Only yes... or no.
His will or nothing. That is the only choice.

Jonah chose. He was free to do so but he was ignorant that
life would crush him apart from The Plan.
Nature would oppose him.
Man would expose him and dispose of him.
Being with him made them subject to his danger.

The wrath of God *does* rest on the disobedient.

You can go against the Plan. You can!
But you will find that to do so is worse than the Plan.

God didn't push Jonah into Nineveh. He never forces. He
merely makes the issues very clear. And the consequences.

What He did was orchestrate the earth so that Jonah could
fathom that it was a crisis of life and death.
Not Nineveh or voyage.
Not this or maybe else that...
but actual life versus literal death.

God IS life. All else is death. With Him is Life and apart from
Him is Death. And that cannot be altered nor diminished.

In the belly of the whale, Jonah recognized the cost of
resistance.

> We seldom comprehend it.
> How blessed is the man who meets the shock of it.

We were created for God...

> not for spouse, nor children. Not for deeds or jobs.
> Not for achievement. Not even for natural abilities.
> For Him... only.

And God is under no obligation to support

> our existence or our agenda
> if it is given to anything other than
> > His Intention,
> > His Idea.

We do have free choice but it is only the

> right to chose death.

God rules fish and sea and wind... and unknowing men.
The flow of life and of events exists for God. Everything
fulfills His wish. All things serve Him and give account to
Him. The great powers of the universe roll in His direction
and to go against that inclusive tide is to call upon yourself
the most miserable drowning.

It isn't God's fault.
He's not to blame when I put my face against the wind and
am pelted by the natural order of things.

Jonah had the exceptional privilege of seeing that one can refuse God but one cannot escape Him.
When Jonah went away, God didn't seek another man.
God tolerates no second choices.
It was Jonah or no one.

We pet this delusion:
When God calls and we lack the grit to say yes, we imagine that to say nothing is to stave off the question. But
no answer is counted as no.
A good substitute is considered a no.
Postponement is reckoned as a no.

Anything other than yes is no. We cannot befuddle Him while we are fogging up our own vision.

You want an ocean between you and the God's city of need?
Then you shall have the ocean. Its depths and terrors.
Its powers and vastness.

In the unimaginable slime of the whale, Jonah made three new choices to rescind his stupid option. Three "I wills."

"I will look again toward His holy temple."
God will not twist our neck toward Himself. It is our job to turn. And the direction of our looking is the direction of our going. This is the first volitional move toward God – to bring your gaze to face His awful penetration of your pitiful self.

Next Jonah determined,
" *I will sacrifice unto Thee*
with the voice of thanksgiving. "
Ingratitude is ever why we leave The Way. We never think
God has done enough for us until we are threatened with its
loss.

And thanksgiving is the willing sacrifice of the man who has
come to an ended life that will not die. In the end we will all
have the shameful poverty of possessing nothing to offer but
praise. Not loyalty, not success, not purity...
a wretched nothingness, and a total devastation.
"I've wrecked it all. All I have left is to praise the astonishing
God who has lowered me below every other form of life. But
I will do that."

To praise God at this juncture *is* a sacrifice!
It's the giving up of understanding,
the surrender of an arrogant mind.
It's the relinquishment of your right to your way,
the death of the will.
It's the oblation of your horror,
the submission of wandering emotions.

Praise cuts through mind, will and emotion
to the bowed knee of pure acquiescence.

Praise is giving God His due
at the expense of my proud control.

It's an acknowledgment that God is right and that
    He is the only one

WHO IS.

The third determination was
    "I will pay that that I have vowed."

Jonah had committed to obedience and gone back on it.
    The cost is ever higher than we count,
      speaking 'yes,' always easier than its carrying out.

It was Jonah's own promise that gave God the right to
corner the man.
        God usurps no rights over us that we have
        not yielded up but He will receive as binding
        those agreements we volunteer.

And it is kind of Him to hold us to our bargain,
    to "help" us be true.

We can't escape Him easily. How comforting!

Were I God, I'd gladly shove out the one
    who didn't want me.

But Love brings the whale, and it is not cruelty.

    Crisis alone makes us regret our disloyalty.
    Ultimate Wisdom knows us well.

Rebellious choices plunge us into the whale
but the choice to be owned sets us free.

With God it's all paradox:
Jonah came out of the whale's control when he gave
up entirely the government of his destiny.

Nothing has the power to hold the man
who has surrendered control to the
Blessed Controller.

Life is an immense tapestry of God's spindle.
Events are woven one upon another, connected by meaning.

No experience is isolated nor is any person.
There are borders that touch and color distant places.
Years may stand between their connection – some never
known – but God is weaving, ever throwing His shuttle over
many threads, pulling them inexorably together in ways that
cannot be undone. We are the threads and we are crossed
upon other yarns, linked together holding each other,
in a final unfathomable tapestry of humanity we call "life."

We all have a Nineveh that waits for us to come, that is our
charge: our city of despairing lives.

We must be willing to be "dyed," spun and strung for
Nineveh. We dare not spoil that immense but secret pattern
by so much as a thread of resistance.

God allows us the great privilege of importance.
But it is only importance insofar as it fits His scheme.
God is going. He *will* crown His Son. He will give Him all.
He will!

He is moving inexorably, unrelentingly toward that end.
We can join His going, but He will not join ours.

There is a fitted role for each. But the fruitless will be
      cast aside and the useless burned.

So no one is indispensable and no one is necessary. Yet all
are invited to be needed... to join the "move."

God will finish.

He is not ultimately dependent on us but
He deigns to reveal His eternal goals to us,
      condescends to share His stage and the
          spoil of His victory.
      To go to Nineveh is an unspeakable privilege.

... and yet under Absolute Sovereignty dwells entirely free
choice.

But Jonah wasn't entirely through with resistance.
      The whale didn't cure him.
        It got him on the right path but not yet of the
          right heart.

He wanted the Ninevite rebels treated with the same
harshness his own revolt had drawn. But the God who
wrung him out had not the same technique for the city.
Rather it was unpunishing grace.

> Jonah deemed that unfair and pouted over it.

Humanity ever stands in judgment of God's ways by
> the standard of its own self-centered justice.

> Jonah had acknowledged that God had won
> but he had yet to concede that God was right.

> I AM… always right.

Daniel

Only those who *bow* to God
have eyes to see His Unmatched Dominion.

All others see a
Dispassionate Weakling.

Marvelous, those persons whose God is Sovereign.
Like Daniel.

He stood at a vulnerable age of 16 and
watched his home and city burn.
Saw his parents, brothers, sisters, friends...
slaughtered.

Carried away to a foreign land of cruel heathen people and
remanded to serve the murderers of his people.

Robbed of his manhood,
stripped down to the barest bone of human existence.

What would you have thought of God in such a plight?

Where would you fit His Sovereignty into this horror?

How would you have assessed His goodness?

Yet to all of it... somehow... Daniel bowed.

When Daniel told the story, this is how he worded it:

"Nebuchadnezzar... came to Jerusalem and
besieged it. <u>And the Lord</u> gave Jehoiakim king of Judah into
his hand... And he brought them to the land of Sinar, to the
house of his god... "

For Daniel, the Cause behind the cause was God.

If you lose sight of God's ruling hand, your world is in
      automatic chaos. Order – perhaps not
      understanding – but order issues from certainty in
      God's Dominion.

One can only bow to God who knows He is the Power
Behind All,
                Above All.

God didn't give Daniel peace in this abysmal mess.

Daniel's accurate beliefs about God gave him peace.

            God was over all.
            God was good.

We submit to the one we think has power over us. We do.
      We don't fight great power once we see it.

Daniel was to be made a servant.
      That was God's idea and Daniel got in touch with it
         and agreed.
By the long tests of serving, he was groomed to be a ruler,
with vast power over the very ones who captured him.

No man can serve an enemy faithfully or fruitfully.
He must see his enemy as a Divine Instrument.
      For hatred begets hatred, and
      bitterness, bitterness.

To think it is a human being who is dealing with you will make you want to kill that man... and he will know it.
And though you be trustworthy, he will not trust you.
Should you be commendable, he still will never commend you...

This belief about His God, worked through in the hurting places,
> gave Daniel a Great Faith.

And when a crisis came, he could expect His God to not only interpret a dream, but reveal its forgotten pictures.

> "It is He who changes the times and epochs,
> He removes Kings and establishes kings."

To Daniel, He had been "God of heaven," ruler of the unseen. Now He saw Him anew, as "God of my fathers."
Having intervened in their lives, He was available to Daniel also in the practical.
Daniel pulled himself out of his tragedy and stepped into tremendous influence.

Sniveling views of God will leave a man in mediocrity.

Since God was the Unseen Force behind the kings,
> *Daniel had no fights with man.*
He didn't love his cruel kings because they endeared themselves. He met each with reverence, who were cruel heathens, because they were God-appointed.

The staggering proof of his mettle was that he was esteemed by a king whose condemnation he announced and then honored by that king's enemy.

What man is there, so enduring?

Blessed by kings to whom he always delivered bad news, placid conqueror of his killers, in quiet companionship with hungry lions.
Sovereignty serves a man well.

Peace pervades his story.
Peace with authority.
Peace forced on his enemies.

His only discomfiture was in the face of his visions. Those visions! They began with dreams, interpreting enigmas to his kings. But every vision grew in scope, both of future events and
the awesome dominion of God.

His visions predicted downfalls of kings before they fell down. Because he grasped that God was the Author of History, he was given the privilege of seeing the events of history the Author was planning... in detail... beforehand. Long, long beforehand.

Daniel saw visions. Then He saw God on His throne and the Son of Man. Such a view of God... to be envied, to be sought.

Daniel's view was continually changing, expanding.

His names for God implied his moving revelation of Him:

First He called Him   God of Heaven
Ruler of the Unseen

Next he saw Him as   God of Fathers
Ruler of my Ancestors

Then   God of gods
Ruler over other powers

Most High God
Ruler over earth

My God
Ruler over me

Ancient of Days
Ruler of the past

Highest One
Ruler over all

Great and Awesome God
Ruler over His own Word
And even...   Messiah
Ruler over sin

After every crisis, Daniel's light was brighter.

> His God bigger,
> The vision grander,
> And Daniel's personal exaltation
> in exact proportion.

But most to be noted is that at the end of Daniel's record, his magnificent view of God created a striking intimacy between them, not implied in the earlier chapters. God shared His deepest secrets with the man, and Daniel, in poignant passion, called Him over and over...

> O my God.

Potential does not lie in skill alone, for skillful men and women go down.

Potential for eternal worth lies in knowing this:

> "... the Most High is ruler over the realm of mankind, and bestows it on whomever He wishes...
>
> ... it is Heaven that rules."

> Daniel 4:25,26

Nebuchadnezzar

The one who worships himself
is a maniac
and knows it not.

All worship not given to God is at root, the worship of self. You worship what you need, so you are yourself the center of your universe and you, the only motive for all you do.

You are your own lover.

The shocking root of Nebuchadnezzar's insanity was simply and only the displacement of God by the deifying of self.

Nebuchadnezzar decreed the worship of himself. Three Jews refused to bow. Their extraordinary belief was that God could deliver them if He chose to. That massive furnace was no obstacle to *their* God!

Their God ruled over the pompous ruthlessness of little strutting potentates. *And they were not afraid..*

Nebuchadnezzar was a firsthand witness not only to their survival but to the presence of their God in the blaze. For a time he basked in the wonder of that God and gave Him His due. But his dream warned him that he still lusted for God's place.

The man who thinks he has achieved it –
imagines he owns it –
will have a season of bestial humiliation.
That is certain and absolutely inevitable.

God's Ruling Position will not suffer competition. It is holy and unapproachable. While God is approachable, His Position is not.

He is God. All of us are jealous of that. We covet His throne.

The root of our depravity is a likeness to Satan, "I will be as
the most High God." And we will not settle even for that –
being "like" God, equal to Him. We will go yet grander,
     "I will exalt my throne *above* the Most High."
And our hidden idea is that God should be our servant.

That secret thinking is insane.
     Indulge in it for long and madness takes over.

The King reaped a seven year harvest from usurping
dominion:

     … isolation from the company of normal men.
     … a primal beast existence, exposure to the
        elements, until a complete (the number
        seven) recognition came, of the difference
        between self and God.

These are symbols of real experiences:
     of inner desolation and public indignity.

     We will only resign as gods when forced to.
     We can only be shamed off our throne.
     We have to be slammed to the ground of obeisance.
     Our faces must know the lowly taste of grass and our
        likeness to the beasts.
     We have to be drenched with the dew of
        heaven's abandonment
     to ever comprehend its sweeping rule.

The unhinged state lasts until this comprehension is full:
> "you know that the Most High rules in the kingdom
> of men, and gives it to whomever He chooses."

Nebuchadnezzar believed he was king because he was a
noble being, and only he could be such. He had to learn
that he was king because God deigned to make it so and for
no reason in the man himself.

> "the Most High is sovereign over the kingdoms of
> men and gives them to anyone he wishes and sets
> over them the lowliest of men."
> And such was himself...

Nebuchadnezzar's soliloquy is worth pondering:

> "And at the end of the time I, Nebuchadnezzar, lifted
> my eyes to heaven and my understanding returned
> to me; and I blessed the Most High and praised and
> honored Him who lives forever:

> "For his dominion is an everlasting dominion,
> And His kingdom is from generation to generation.
> All the inhabitants of the earth are reputed as
> nothing; He does according to His will in the army of
> heaven and among the inhabitants of the earth.
> No one can restrain His hand Or say to Him, 'What
> have you done?'

> "At the same time my reason returned to me... my
> kingdom... my honor and splendor. I was restored

to my kingdom, and excellent majesty was added to me.

"Now I, Nebuchadnezzar, praise and extol and honor the King of heaven, all of whose works are truth and His ways justice. And those who walk in pride He is able to put down."

Nebuchadnezzar understood who he was *and* who God was and the unbridgeable gap between the two.

When he took his place, stayed within its God-ordained bounds, he was blessed, even exalted.
God can give much to the man
who will let Him have His throne.

In the practice of life, if we try to orchestrate the immediate universe, praying that God will obey us by the support of our agenda,
we have become Nebuchadnezzar.

There is a pitiful unawareness to this control.
To be blind is one thing but when you are blind to your blindness, you are dangerous and must be stopped.

And as Nebuchadnezzar discovered, God is up to the job.

Only God's Sovereign Interference
can convince you of...
sovereignty.

Me

Many know Him as Forgiveness,
some know Him as Love, Truth, so on.
But few know God as... God.

I walked with furious "whys," buried far below in
                  secret tortures.

My mother died an awful death when I was 15, devastating
me into a mean and barren world from what had been a
warm hearth. That young suffering cried out for
                  reasonable explanation… to satisfy me.

A great conflict raged in hidden places. I knew it not, till
God revealed it. This was the conflict:

    Who took my mother?
                Was it God? Oh, no, God is
                good… couldn't have been God.

    My mother's death was
    so bad for me.
                But God is ultimately in control.
                Or is He?

    Satan's evil force? Yes,
    No doubt.
                Was it God's will?

    How could it be?
                Or was it her fault?

    It had been a long and sweating question…
    with no solution.

When finally He pulled that "why" from its dark musing
place, He answered. But notice please, He didn't explain.

"I hold the keys to hell and to death.
Yes, Martha, I took your mother just as you suspected.

But there is no contradiction between my Goodness
and her death...
I am God. And I am good. And I took your mother,
therefore your mother's death was good.

Now praise Me."

So I thanked Him for that which had
wrecked me, for what I had resisted for years. Somehow it
was easy.

Still no explanation why.
Just that it was good, for my good, because He is good.

His sweet answer resolved my division, healed my pain.
And somehow I was deeply satisfied.
I hadn't needed to know "why" after all.

I had needed to know if God was irrevocably in charge.
If I was really vulnerable to life and evil... to anything that
would want to harm me. If as a sheltered, rather helpless
youngster, my world could almost overnight be ruined, then

it must follow that anything might happen, any horrible prospect was a possibility.

Did I have any protection? Any security?

My moorings had been shaken. An explanation of why it had happened would not have answered my real need:
the need to know if life could shake me unmercifully while God watched in indifference or
worse still, helplessness.

The answer was I AM. And that was what I most needed to know. He WAS God. He really was.

A God – not a Judging Observer but a
Very Present Force.

I walked out of the buried sickness my lonely 'why'
had caused.

For it was not her death that made my agony, nor did any related suffering… but my failure to comprehend the God above and behind it all.
My deep question was not really of events (as I imagined) but of His Innate Goodness and His Overriding Power.
After all the errors of man and their consequences;
after all obvious evil has had its way,
was God still God? Did He have the final say?

I saw that His Goodness and His Power were so vast that
      no evil, no suffering has

      any power to harm me in His realm.

All disaster is swallowed up in His supremacy and becomes,
      not just benign, but beneficial!

The problem was not the suffering – it was my separation
from God while I was in it. As soon as I dug it up –
      no, as soon as He dug it up –
      and put it inside His Sovereignty, the pain was gone.

When one has no longer any pain in suffering,
      what matters the suffering?

The transformation of those beliefs about
      Who He IS made me whole,
      and I saw in my daily living, the proof of it.

Giddy, incredulous, I knew that God had given me the key to the healing of man's inner pain. I sensed I had touched, not just my own solution, but an eternal cure. An audacious claim for sure!

But one of which I was, and would remain,
    absolutely certain.

    A truth which was crystal clear and
      undeniable in His Word.

The key: a single belief and a simple response, based on scripture:

    God is sovereign.
    I thank Him.

    For

      God is... and He *is* God!

Romans One

Inch by defiant inch, we build
our suicidal ruin by forsaking God.
He is not to be blamed
when we chase the darkness
and catch it.

It was 12 years before I found the scripture that presented
the truth I had lived and by which I had been made secure.
It was Romans 1:21 and following…

what may be known about God is plain to them
because God has made it plain to them. For
since the creation of the world God's invisible
qualities – his eternal power and divine nature –
have been clearly seen, being understood from
what has been made, so that men are without excuse.

His eternal power… that is sovereignty
His divine nature… that is goodness.
These are written in nature, clear in
creation. Visible and unmistakable.

For although they knew God, they neither
glorified him as God nor gave thanks to him,

God is obvious. Plain. Our response
should be awe at His power and
gratitude for His goodness. To fail in
these responses is to begin a
downward spiral to certain and
unending disaster.

but their thinking became futile

Thoughts void of His sovereignty
and goodness make a mind that is
ineffective.

and their foolish hearts were darkened.

> The mind feeds the heart its futility. And
> the heart begins to spew emotions of
> darkness and stupidity.

Although they claimed to be wise,
they became fools

> Empty minds make hearts in secret,
> foolish. Soon the fool goes public and
> thinks his dim wit is wise.

and exchanged the glory of the immortal God
for images made to look like mortal man and
birds and animals and reptiles.

> We must have a god. To spurn the real
> One is to fabricate an absurd counterfeit,
> dead and useless.

Therefore God gave them over in the sinful
desires of their hearts to sexual impurity for
the degrading of their bodies with one another.

> Sexual immorality is the evidence (and
> the result) of forsaking the God of All,
> who IS pleasure and fulfillment.

They exchanged the truth of God for a lie

> God is not only Truth but He is Reality.
> And He is the only
> source of it.
>
> Where God is… Truth is.
> Where God isn't… the lie lives
> instead.

*and worshipped and served created
things rather than the Creator –
who is forever praised.*

> If you don't serve the Creator who
> created you to be His, you will slave for
> the things He created.

*Because of this, God gave them over to
shameful lusts. Even their women exchanged natural
relations for unnatural ones. In the same way the men
also abandoned natural relations with women and were
inflamed with lust for one another. Men committed
indecent acts with other men,*

> Down and down, worse and worse. God
> spurned is Satan enthroned. And this
> master spawns his obsessive perversion
> in you to the loss of your own
> magnificent gender.

and received in themselves the
due penalty for their perversion.

There are terrible consequences to
twisting His order to feed our lusts. A
penalty due us, that we chose and
fostered.

Furthermore, since they did not think
it worthwhile to retain the knowledge of
God, he gave them over to a depraved
mind, to do what ought not to be done.

Mental illness is the choice we make to
refuse what we know... that
God is good and
God is God.

They have become filled with every kind of wickedness,
evil, greed and depravity. They are full of envy, murder,
strife, deceit and malice. They are gossips, slanderers,
God-haters, insolent, arrogant and boastful; they invent
ways of doing evil; they disobey their parents, they are
senseless faithless, heartless, ruthless.

Complex problems and heinous sins
have two simple, basic roots: one, the
refusal to recognize the all powerful God
and two, the absence of simple gratitude
for who He is.

God Is Good

God is great, God is good,
     little children know.
Adults have had that knowledge destroyed.

Tell me God is sovereign and I quake.
Tell me He is also good and I relax.

His sovereignty is made tolerable by His
immeasurable goodness.

In fact the word good is insipid when used of His goodness.
His "good" is beyond vocabulary.

When Jesus was called "good master" He said

"Why call ye me good?
There is only one who is good,
The Father in Heaven."

"There is only one good"... That excludes every other
appearance of good. In fact, according to that statement,
there is

no good *except* God.

All that man produces is not good. The noble acts, the
heroic deeds, the generous behavior –
all the good of man – is not good. Not true good.

His goodness is incomprehensible to us. And the enemy's
favorite device is to cruelly blind us as to that goodness...
to present proof it doesn't exist and leave us in the fearful
dilemma of that.

"Holy" isn't usually in question concerning God. Holy we
can buy. But good, really good, ah, that is another matter.

God's goodness is vindicated by His restoration not only of Job, but of Job's recalcitrant friends who received God's high disapproval.

His goodness is seen in His divine plan for Joseph. He was all along, in secret design, preparing him for good, even splendid things: the rulership of Egypt and the salvation of his people, the very ones who caused him such unjust suffering. God was even good to those treacherous brothers!

> "I know the plans I have for you, plans
> to prosper you and not to harm you, to
> give you a hope and a future"

> Jeremiah 29:11

God always has His plans: exciting, splendid
orders for the future.

To Daniel He gave the unimaginable rulership of his captor's nation! And more than that to Daniel He gave a place of significance in all human ages and throughout eternity.

Abraham, He made rich in the very incident of his disloyalty to Sarah... made rich by the king to whom his lie caused great suffering. God's goodness knows no limits except those we create.

God can bless the one who knows He is God
and doesn't object.

But most poignant and most inscrutable is the offering of
His own Son to hideous suffering. Why? So that He could
freely bestow His goodness on mankind who deserved only
His wrath. We can never take it in. Rarely is even one of us
able to approach receiving it. We weigh His goodness by our
standard: by the sensual, by peace or happiness, by the
things He gives. And by that external we judge Him.

> We have no real vision of His vast good,
> His complete goodness.

God's goodness is in a realm of pure motive, the motive of
His own love in the face of our unworthiness of it. It is
absolute integrity, impeccable character, wherein He never
can be accused of wrong or even the slightest injustice.

He is not the "God of feeding the five thousand."
He is the "God of twelve baskets left over!"

He has not withheld one thing from us, and even
beyond what we need,

> He has given everything He has, even to
> the rulership of the world, a throne with His Son!

Do you understand? He has withheld nothing from us!
> "every spiritual blessing in heavenly places… "
> "… all things are yours."

"He who did not spare His own son. Will He not freely
        give us all things?"
The problem is never, ever with God.
The problem only is in our receptiveness.
We buy the ancient lie –
        God is not good, as proven by what He has withheld.

So we banish our bitter selves from His lavishness.

We hold onto our transgressions by failure of admission and
when we don't experience His outpouring we say He isn't
outpouring.

In our proud destitution, we would rather die than need
Him. And in our insane independence, we would rather fail
than give Him the credit for our victory.

The beggarly alone find themselves in the
        wondrous kingdom.

                    I AM... good.

Sovereignty Shared

God gives a place
in His own dominion to the one
doesn't try to out God God.

Though God is sovereign, having unchallenged dominion,
He limits His involvement to our invitation.

Many, so tragically many, of God's purposes fall to the
ground. Things are not always as He would perfectly have
them. But that is not His fault – it is ours. We are given the
most incredible responsibility – that of changing the world
through prayer, not by our "fixing," not by our ruling, but
by the opposite, being involved in only one power – His!
And that great dynamic obtained through prayer to watch
Him intervene in man's futility.

*God has given man the chance to have power
over events.*

Only for the sustaining of His will, only that! Not
independent power, not for man to decide, to rule, to 'be.'

Humanity is meant to be the very instrument
of God's own sovereignty.

Each person has as Esther did, a moment of history, where
one's birth comes to its divine design – 'for such a time as
this'.

Even so He will obtain His ultimate purpose. He will. And
such is His brilliance that He will use even man's rebellion
to do so.

"The wrath of man shall praise Him."

So sovereignty cannot lull us into passivity. "Ah, well, what will be will be."

Humanity drools for power.

The whole world is embroiled in an obsession with power. The quest for money is really for the power money gives. Nations vie for power. Families struggle to gain power over each other. And the work place is a place of the scratch and fight to get domination. Wherever man is, there is the contest, the fray over power.

Man wants God's place of government but God has given a different power to mankind, a monumental place of dominion by acquiescence. In resorting to prayer, abdicating the human powers which are all illegitimate, man picks up his intended power – the power to change events without participating in them, without exerting so much as a word. Prayer alone, seeking only God's will, brings God's will into dominion over humanity's stupid mess.

Jesus' term in the wilderness was a contest of power.
      The temptation was to use real but
            illegitimate power.

The first was power over matter. "Change the stone into bread." Jesus preferred to suffer, even to starve, rather than manipulate matter.

The next was power over God. "Jump – and let the angels catch you." Step out beyond yourself and force God's hand. Jesus would not jump until and unless God directed so. He gave up His own influence over God... forever.

The third was power over man, the temptation to govern man rather than serve him.

These are the three categories of man's ambition: Supremacy over
              matter, God and man.

Jesus abdicated those human powers. In doing so, He relied only on the Power of the Most High, gained through prayer...

              and let God be Himself,

              The Great I AM.

Pictures of Jesus

Empathy is a bond forged only
by sharing the same fire,
and this Jesus did…
He entered the fire of every person.

The characters of the Old Testament are real.
Some of their ordeals are like ours –
they look like our wrestlings with God and
they ring of our opposition to the life He oversees
So we view some of them from personal eyes.

But there is One who relates to all those struggles.
They are really pictures of Jesus.
As God, we see Jesus in His perfect surrender,
His flawless obedience.
But in the peculiar prison of humanity,
He faced it all.

He lived through Joseph's rejection by his brothers.
He faced the weakness of Abraham,
the wrestlings of Habakkuk.

He suffered misunderstanding of arrogant friends
and mortal pain just like Job.
He probably lost a parent to death… just like me…

Jesus knows the feelings of our weakness, the
futility of our sweat…

Jesus faced it all. Some we know about.
Most we don't.
The amazing fact, given to us in scripture is that
He was tempted in all things just as we are,
yet He didn't sin.

The Bible says, "in every way."

All of human experience in some measure,
in ways unwritten,
by secret struggling,
was His experience.

What a God!
Sovereign and powerful in the heavenlies,
yet put His Son in our miserable moccasins
so that God could actually live the human dilemma!

All of it.

Including... Yours.

I AM

All and Only

For copies of this book, tape lists, other publications or additional information, please write to:

Shulamite Publishing
P.O. Box 10
Suches, Georgia 30572

or call:

1-888-355-5373

Or reach us on the Internet at:

http://www.Shulamite.com

CHURCH LIFE
An Open Letter to House Church Leaders (Edwards)
When the Church Was Led Only By Laymen (Edwards)
Beyond Radical (Edwards)
How to Meet Under the Headship of Jesus Christ (Edwards)
The Open Church (Rutz)
Revolution, The Story of the Early Church (Edwards)
The Silas Diary (Edwards)
The Titus Diary (Edwards) 1999
Church Unity (Litzman, Nee, Edwards)
Let's Return to Church Unity (Kurosaki)
Climb the Highest Mountain (Edwards)
The Torch of the Testimony (Kennedy)
Passing of the Torch (Chen)
Going to Church in the First Century (Banks)
When the Church Was Young (Loosley)
Rethinking Elders (Edwards)
Overlooked Christianity (Edwards)

ON THE DEEPER CHRISTIAN LIFE
How to Live by the Highest Life (Edwards)
The Secret to the Christian Life (Edwards)
The Inward Journey (Edwards)
Bone of His Bone (Huegel)
The Centrality of Jesus Christ (T. Austin-Sparks)
The House of God (T. Austin-Sparks)
The Ultimate Intention (Fromke)
Final Steps in Christian Maturity (Guyon)

LIBRARY OF SPIRITUAL CLASSICS
Practicing His Presence (Lawrence/Laubach)
Experiencing the Depths of Jesus Christ (Guyon)
Union With God (Guyon)
The Seeking Heart (Fenelon)
The Spiritual Guide (Molinos)
The Song of the Bride (Guyon)

SEEDSOWERS PUBLISHING HOUSE
800-645-2342